Homage to
Edgar Allan Poe

Books by Dave Smith

POETRY
Dream Flights
Goshawk, Antelope
Cumberland Station
The Fisherman's Whore
Mean Rufus Throw Down

LIMITED EDITIONS
Blue Spruce
In Dark, Sudden with Light
Drunks
Bull Island

CRITICISM
The Pure Clear Word:
Essays on the Poetry of James Wright

NOVEL
Onliness

Homage to Edgar Allan Poe

POEMS BY DAVE SMITH

Louisiana State University Press
Baton Rouge and London
1981

Designer: Joanna Hill
Typeface: Electra
Typesetter: G & S Typesetters, Inc.
Printer and Binder: Thomson-Shore, Inc.

The author gratefully acknowledges the editors of the following magazines, in which many of these poems first appeared, sometimes in slightly different form and under different titles: *Agni Review* ("Juniper, Wyoming," "Backyard, Under the Wasatch Ridge, at Dusk"), *American Poetry Review* ("A Man's Daughter," "Lovers, September," "Homage to Edgar Allan Poe," "Night of the Chickens, North of Joplin"), *American Scholar* ("Under a White Shawl of Pine"), *Antaeus* ("Season of Light, Season of Sickness"), *Canto* ("Documentary"), *Chariton Review* ("Wedding Song"), *Cimarron Review* ("The Plum Tree," "A Stillness in the Heart"), *Kansas Quarterly* ("The Sinner"), *Nation* ("Pond"), *Northwest Review* ("Sometime I Think I Will Ride into Saint Louis"), *Quarterly West* ("Homecoming Parade, That Music," "Discovering Obscenities on Her Wall," "The Abused [Hansel and Gretel]"), *Quest/80* ("Men with Women," "First Star," "Silver Maples and Mulberry"), *Paris Review* ("Sax Man," "Waking Under Spruce with My Love"), *Poetry* ("The Soft Belly of the World"), *Pearl* ("Under Dogwood, Under Pine, Under Spruce"), *Prairie Schooner* ("Reading the Books Our Children Have Written"), *Sam Houston Literary Journal* ("Starlight, Starbright"), *Western Humanities Review* ("Two Songs for the Round of the Year," "Against Lawyers," "Oak Leaf, a Midnight Dream," "Utah Prospective," "Elk Ghosts: A Birth Memory"). "Something Is Missing," "Negative: The Little Engine That Could," "What Happened This Morning" were first published in *In Dark, Sudden with Light* by Croissant & Co., Booksellers, Athens, Ohio, 1977. "Portrait of a Lady (p. 63); © 1978 The New Yorker Magazine, Inc. "A Day with No Clouds" first appeared in *Three Rivers Poetry Journal*, © 1977 by Three Rivers Press.

I am especially grateful to the University of Utah for a David P. Gardner Research Award for 1979, which afforded me time to complete this collection.

Library of Congress Cataloging in Publication Data

Smith, Dave, 1942–
    Homage to Edgar Allan Poe.

    I. Title.
PS3569.M5173H6   811'.54   81–4767
ISBN 0-8071-0873-1   AACR2
ISBN 0-8071-0874-X (pbk.)

*This book is dedicated to
John and Jeri Spears*

Contents

Sometime We Will Ride into Saint Louis

"You are nineteen?" he asked.
"Yes, signor maggiore."
"You have ever been in love?"
"How do you mean, signor maggiore?"
"In love—with a girl?"
"I have been with girls."
"I did not ask you that. I asked
if you had been in love—with a girl."

Ernest Hemingway,
Men with Women

Two Songs
for the Round
of the Year

Blue apple of the night,
apple of fear,
apple of peace,
the small leaves tear
and hiss in their fright
and the big moon screams

in its rut of the darkness.
Why is it hung there
on the starred rug
like a toy you hear
broken and distant? Why shrug
so? Have you not been blessed?

The boy who was once a man
thinks of no question
as he stands blued
by the dark that beckons.
He lifts his hand
and blots out the moon.

You have done this, long ago.
Perhaps you remember.
And recall that toy
now, and a night off far
watching apples as a boy.
They danced in the wind-blow.

Surely, you thought, by light
all will be torn.
And the leaves were, but
the apple held, shorn
as your heart's delight
nakedly crying where? why? what?

Only what is never answered,
nor ever is why.
Stand there and watch.
Small leaves rip and die.
You are the moon's catch.
Lift your hand, go on. Remember.

Christmas Memory

Children, what have you put by
that this night on a shelf
of the future your hand
comes to remember, that
with it I come back to you?

I see the way you are sitting
in the blue fume of the tree,
stilled by toys, the apple
core tenuously held,
the milk glass emptied, white.

This hour I have prowled alone
in the sleeping family house.
I hear your slow breathing,
brothers and sisters. A clock
hums like water through pipes

that spill in the hardening dark.
I have locked each door, pulled
all the plugs, tried to find
the star that drifts on the floor.
Unawake, you stirred and kissed me.

Why then should shadow startle?
Yet I looked, as in your moment
you must look, and out there
saw the great graceful Buck
that you will know in my telling.

I do not guess why he has come,
but think of you, this moment
when turned to the cold glass
of night you cry, Father?—
No answer. There is none.

Long, like a spirit of earth,
he stood unblinking. I saw
in time the ghost shape
my face held and within it
his shape, tall, brave, lifeless,

as if I had only thought him there.
When he leaped I felt how live
the family house is, fathers
rising in the breath of children,
and sat at love's tree to tell you

Here, forever, here—

The Stories
of Our Daughters

Backyard, Under the
Wasatch Ridge, at Dusk

How hard it is to say a thing straight
with minutes boiling
like eggs on the stove.

The door is wide open but I don't even move.
Out there the dog zig-zags,
led by his nose
through inaudible light.

He will stop forever to stare down a blade of grass.
He will say nothing important softly
to everything that leaps.

The drone of sirens is rising
up our hill, a daughter
cries somewhere.

Inside our anonymous houses we drift back along
the deepening blue and uncut grasses
of our lives, wanting to move
but just looking,

just looking—

as if far down in those shy blue tunnels
a mouth opens, amazed
we have come at last,

and the right, final word tries to leap
over the sudden shoulder of breath.

for Bruce Weigl

9

She tries to call them down,
quicknesses of air.
They bitch and scorn,
they roost away from her.

It isn't that she's brutal.
She's just a girl. Worse,
her touch is total.
Her play is dangerous.

Darkly they spit each at each,
from tops of pine and spruce.
Her words are shy and sweet,
but it's no use.

Ragged, blue, shrill,
they dart around like boys.
They fear the beautiful
but do not fly away.

In the far corner of yard,
next to our secret garden,
the spruce shadow
leans away and reveals
her coiled body.
She pretends to sleep
where the boys have gone
whistling off like birds.
The ground under her is
cool, and is not yet
a man's pillowing arm.
The spruce understands
for a while she is
its gift and itself
leans back to whisper
its big-whiskered dream.
The spruce, oh, is
blue like her eyes,
and dark, and fatherly.
It keeps watch like a dog,
snarling at intruders
no matter what it hears.

11

Down the hill the little boy runs
toward the black-roofed school.
Faces like bruised tangerines,
chasing him, three girls

go by as if winged, bodies
slender as summer's insects.
They are gay, but their eyes
are deep pits, dark and quick.

If he stopped, faced them,
like the angels of Heaven
they would crash over him,
and no breath of the sun

could repair what his flesh was.
Each morning from a slit
in the city, like a spruce,
he springs, takes the first step,

but they are there, still, quiet,
radiant as the lemony day
we ourselves will rise
in, unable to look away

as the heart is unable to cease
and yet remain a heart.
We watch them go, three,
and one gone to the dark.

Beside us our small daughter
stands, her shoulders drawn,
pulsing, who leans to the door,
cold-cracked, blistered by sun.

Her name and those relentless words stunned.
It sprawled yellow among blue oaths
lugged home from school where boys revealed
what only the world's wall, and Spring's, had known.

This stained cheek was ours, harshly summoned.
She gleamed more than the dew on drying hay
where boys waited to run her to ground.
She had no answer. She cannot say why.

Impatient, I watched her deny all she did.
She tilted her head as mockingbirds do
to see how an unknown thing might be said.
Whatever she saw stirred and would not go

out of her head. Like a wild thing she looked
beyond me, afraid, blinking. Then she shook.

Dark settles. I wait for my kiss goodnight,
remembering how, once released, she swirled
up as if unchanged, ignorant of fate.
I saw her erase what the boys gave her,

and clean up her room and take a hot bath.
For hours she's studied to learn by heart
her first book's colorful lessons and truths.
Now she must kiss and lie down in the dark.

Lord, while she can let her deny it all.
Grant her grace in love and yellow letters,
give her a song and dance before these walls.
Give her years before a bright boy beds her.

In love, not ignorance, let her be blessed
to write joy's name and to dirt be witness.

Stiffly at first, then with less awkwardness the slim
thigh-like stems surge up from the earth,
and the white follicles curl like long hair,
and the full-breasted blossom sways,
a kind of bell that is all day ringing and ringing,

except we can't hear anything, my daughter and I. She wants
to know what this is, so I mumble something about
growth and she, shyly, says it takes a long time
and many seeds don't get to be plants. School
has done this to her. This is a movie
I answer, but she says only "Oh it's pretend,

a story without people that you can't understand
even when you see it." What is *it*, I ask,
becoming her teacher. You know, you know, is all I get,
as we begin the wrestling, me trying not to hurt her,
those fragrant hands jabbing up at my eyes.

The Plum Tree

White and nearly perfect
now, a vision in air
where winter had been.
I did not see it defect—

like my girl grown at top
of the stairs, curled
into time and beauty,
the daughter not yet

lost, though her voice falls
lower, admitting its secret.
It comes from that ground
long forgotten, or almost

forgotten, for it is not.
Love's darkness comes back,
sweet and razor-quick,
a grassy place intimate

where gusts now deliver
rains of white brilliance.
Somewhere a bird speaks
as if its throat will tear.

My child listens and I, late,
hear the shadowed dirt
yielding to plum and love's
remembered ache.

Pond

The soft forgiving ooze of the pond's bottom,
that cool fluid move through the toes
when you step out just beyond roots,
through weeds, into that black slough

that the dream has warned is love's terror:
to stand in this abiding ruck among shells
maybe of ancestors, maybe of daughters,
is to feel the flesh in the world

and to think of the last time you were in love,
the vertigo and skidding pale sky,
the lily's gentle, perfect moves,
that slippery beauty, that quick eternity.

Woman and Man

Come this leaf-littered pair, along a road
I have no reason to be on but am, smiling
under the sun that will soon drop like a rock,
both seeming not to know the dark waits
in the dirt where they were and in the sky
hovering with night. When they pass I stop,
mumbling my hello, the owl of my envy
grinding limbs with tight silver talons.
I must bless what they will walk to and sing
the far-falling disaster of stars that burn
out of the brightness they will never escape.

From the hill's high crown, it looked like a plane of grass
but this was light's trick, and thick as nightmare, the plunge
of wind and shadow disguising the lake. She told me how last
week she'd thought the calendar's red X was wrong, and lunged

ahead, blithe on that dangerous ground. The algae lay dark in drifts
under clear water. Slowly the light changed upward and the black
of storm shrank around that place. We stood like birds against wind
ripping the silver of water. Rain beat at our faces and backs.

The few words we had, we spoke and left. Somewhere we heard trunks
bending and keening. Then stillness. Then sky went gold and her face
sang up for a circling loon. I am a man with a man's good luck.
I saw her kneel for the tender crop at the black place.

I watched the water clear, watched her glitter. How green all was,
and overhead a bird's white belly wheeled like a moon for love.

Someone is smoking in the darkness
on the porch of the land.
Somewhere is falling the last
light-edged word, and wind
walks in from the west.

Hurry, you can feel the absence.
Hurry, call like a storm:
"It's me!" Use present tense,
for time is now the form
the surf takes, and it's urgent.

That star is not smoke. It deceives.
You are no child to declare
again, "But I'm not ready."
What, then, of surf and step-flare
always the same? "It's me—"

Why does that smoker on stairs not answer?
Is it wind? Is it distance? Is it anger?

Her face rounded, a pouch without bones, appears
in the ordinary way, boarding the bus.

Everyone looks, the coin drops, a silver tinkle.
Then her coat, the gift of a sailor,

is falling open on her throat's light flesh.
The grin of an otter, maybe, a child,
and you are startlingly sure

she would never hide a thing from you. Face
ordinary as raw wind which has rubbed it all day,
she sits where sunlight rakes over her.

Where were you going when you saw her, you
with the sudden belly of terror?

Somewhere a woman sits in a pearl light, the skin
of her cheeks, once flashing, turned to dust.
Maybe you will never come back.

At the end of an alley this ordinary girl's father
drools in his sleep and seems to be someone
you are certain she cannot love any longer.

His daughter, dressed in that long black, digs
her nails into your hands, and someone whispers.

But who says *Forget him, my beauty, forget him?*

The Abused (Hansel and Gretel)

Sometimes, eating my mush, I think: Oh wrong!
I should have kissed the one shoved face-forward.
In my dream she's that darling with her song
black as the wood's belly, and tufted warts
cushy and bristling. A lifer like me
remembers bad, forgets things good, nightmare's
kid, but she was a looker in truth, sleek
tongued. I don't know why we did it to her.

We are all innocent: I remember
there was this girl. We went into the woods.
We had a fine time but one of us burned.
In the dream I kiss her. It's always good.
Had a sister once. She moved on, married.
Oh lost! That looker's tongue, I still feel it.

for Miller Williams

21

Against Lawyers

The practice of exacting wergeld was abandoned when Roman law substituted the principle of justice for that of reparation and revenge.
THE READER'S ENCYCLOPEDIA

Now I lay me down to sleep.
Steel me dark and darling powers.
I pray the Lord my soul to keep.
Stars help me reap, and with rancor.

If I should die before I wake
I pray the Lord my soul to take
and breed me sons in rattlesnakes.

Give us time and vision not to cower.

I pray this curse against all lawyers
who'd milk our sons and steal our daughters.
One got my wife and got my boon.
I drink to him and bay at the moon.

The night's my cell, gun, knife, and fang.
Make me, I pray Lord, wergeld's one man gang.

for James Whitehead

22

Desks

Piled on a loading dock where I walked,
    student desks battered, staggered
by the dozens, as if all our talk
    of knowledge was over,

as if there'd be no more thin blondes
    with pigtails, no math, no art,
no birds to stare at. Surplus now, those moulds
    we tried to sleep in, always hard

so it wouldn't be pleasant and we'd fall
    awake in time for the one question
with no answer. Quiet as a study hall,
    this big place, this final destination,

oblivious to whatever the weather is,
    hearing the creak of the wind's weight.
The desks are leg-naked, empty, as if
    we might yet come, breathless, late.

And all that time I thought of the flames
    I hadn't guessed, of a blonde
I had loved for years, how the names
    carved one into another would

all scar out the same, blunt, hard, in blue
    searing, like love's first pain.
I stood there like a child, scared, new,
    bird-eyed, not knowing why I came.

A woman pours water from a yellow rubber pail, gives
water to plants receptive as children.
Cornered, I watch from the floor where
on my belly, twice as long

as children on either side, I blink at the future.
Do they hear it, the children, as I do, water
gurgling down to the roots, the blind
shove of the numinous

thin tendrils with no dream of wind or dark ice?
Three of us lift a blank face that drones
over the track of momentary hope,
but we are not speaking

about roots clamped in blind pots where any hand,
if it wanted to, could make a sound like love.
We have just heard of despair, engines,
a climb as sweet as water.

Reading the Books
Our Children Have Written

They come into this room while the quail are crying to huddle up,
the canyon winds just beginning. They pass my big brown desk,
their faces damp and glistening like the first peaches washed,
and offer themselves to be kissed. I am their father still,
I kiss them, I say *See you tomorrow!* Their light steps fade
down the stairs, what they are saying like the far stars
shrill, hard to understand. They are saying their father
writes a book and they are in it, for they are his children.
Then they lie in their beds waiting for sleep, sometimes singing.

Later I get up and go down in darkness and find the hour they played
before they were scrubbed, before they brought me those faces.
There on the floor I find the stapled pages, the strange mild
countenances of animals no one has ever seen, the tall dark man
who writes an endless story of birds homeless in the night. They have
numbered every page, they have named each colorful wing.
They have done all this to surprise me, surprising themselves.
On the last lined yellow page, one has written *This is a poem.*
Under this the other one has answered. *See tomorrow.*

Homage to
Edgar Allan Poe

I. The Hotel: Old Point Comfort

When I was six, grandparents brought me here in a Hudson green
as the drowned mountains of the Chesapeake.

We passed through the gates of Fort Monroe to the sea-wall.
With a mound of string and a rotting chicken neck
I tried for the great Blue crab.

They walked the promenade before the towered hotel.
Their war was over.
Now and then I would see them
gathered in knots, men in strange brown suits,
women holding pastel skirts that bloomed in the wind.

Like flowers they would bend to me, smudged with tears.
It was 1948. They were impatient,
ready to go somewhere.

Once, holding hands, they took me up the wide gray stairs.

Waiters scurried in white silk shirts, in suits sleek and black.
Through mustached lips, they spoke softly
and the candles kept all dim
as if the war endured.

Later, we stood and watched the steamer *Pocahontas* slide to Baltimore.

Tonight the smell of crab steams in the air, and the rank
moon draws, at low tide, the mud's body forth.
Here, in 1849, Miss Ingram of Norfolk
heard Poe read "Ulalume."

"There were many persons on the long verandas
that surrounded the hotel,
but they seemed remote and far away,"
she wrote.

In the Hudson going home that night, I was buried
between the old ones, their bodies ripe.
Around us night congealed.

There was the steady blue of the Chesapeake
and headlights clawing the dark ahead
but I was too small to see much,
and frightened by the voice on the radio

declaiming "The Shadow Knows."

II. Nekkid

Why was I there?

Fourteen, lank, dark, marked
by appetities that seeped up like convictions,
shipped off to summer camp near Richmond,

not Robbie or Bill, his drowned brother,
I would not launch myself stark *nekkid*
from the sycamore, however summer blistered,
however welcome the pool
of the James.

Lord, I read Poe, suffered, at near anything flared,
thus was let alone, as weird.

Past an old wooden bridge, beyond a rag-top Ford
parked by a syrupy creek, wearing black jeans and T-shirt
already clammed with sweat, I climbed a path
and came, that morning, clear

to a humped outcropping of fieldstone with a view
of the valley, the river, and Poe's city.

Below,
more dark distance straight down than I'd ever dreamed.

I edged out as far as I dared, as if to the lip of truth,
shaking in the fresh wind,
afraid of the fall, driven by youth.

I saw Richmond, smoke layering its ancestral depths.
From hundred-year-old windows here and there
the sun's light leaped back
from warehouses and wharves,
taverns, towers, sleeping rooms of whores,

probably. Not hard to believe Poe came from this.

In my mind a manly city, state, what I was,
not this maze of green, this camp country,
trees whose names I wouldn't memorize.
In mid-air I saw two hawks
sail darkly in a thermal lift.
I smelled sap rising in the hard hollows.

        I climbed because I wanted to *see*,
and not just the close-lapping slit
of the river—I wanted to look at all there
spread-eagled, the nearly white streaks
                of foam

spit along the pink bumps and ridges,
the thin peninsulas and archipelagos.

I knew that down there the boys went *nekkid*
and I would sometime, maybe.
             Robbie's brother
is in it yet, in that stink,
his scream handed to the air.
               You would think
time or something would tell why we are
compelled to return
to places and moments
where wreckage occurred.

Climbing down to those boys I'd left slick-haired,
reeking with the James, in bronze leaves,
I heard it, that scoring wheeze of pleasure.
I stopped, uncertain in shadow, timid,
still hearing Robbie's brother
maybe.
   The cry of this is the cry of that.

Her legs waved naked in the air.
As pale as I was, he was buried,
while underneath her face went from flat

to a grin. She grinned as he hurried,
then I heard his voice,
    "You sneaking son of a bitch."

I ran, certain this meant my throat cut,
busting through bush, my body ripping vines loose,
ripped to red tracks, and wasn't caught
unless you could count lying awake, shaken
nightlong by each leaf and weed
making a sound, unless
you count that appalling, grinning face

I carted home that summer, the face of Richmond
that creaks like the bridge I clattered over,
far more than nekkid,
wishing I was Robbie's drowned brother.

Wishing I was not weird, not in love with her,
not a son of a bitch

flung like spit into the universe.

III. Nightcrawlers

I was thinking of an old crabber, moss-backed, a figure
who drained the bottle and tossed it
as he trolled in toward the wharf
lit yellow, lonely.

His hands tying up the 24 foot scow would be luminous,

and luminous his crabs, bubbling, in the crown of the barrel.

I wanted to see him one more time, this man of the people
I'd put in my poems, and his boat only a silhouette
on the skid of darkness where
water scuffed at the reeds.

Under stars that glowed like a small town sitting to supper,
I took off my shoes and walked again.
Had I invented
the raw sheen of wharf and debris and his face?

Deep black grass, and wet, took me through the night's yards
where many crawlers shouldered slowly. I felt them
underfoot and, as if they entered my body,
feel them now, wet and slick,
though this is imagination.

Phrenologists call it Veneration, *Poe wrote.*

I stood at the wharf's flank among bobbing and shunting hulls
waiting for whoever he would be to materialize.
In one of the hulls half-buried
with its cargo of water, I saw
worms of light alive.

He would be, I thought, the hard-shelled diver of deeps,
thinker and doer who would know me.

Slowly he wedged himself into a dark slip, delicate
with his crabs, his pots, his tools, boots.
The rest he flung down in the gut
of the scow's wheelhouse,
not loaded, heroic or miserable
as I had conceived, only a crabber.

*As regards the greater truths, men oftener err by seeking them
at the bottom than at the top.*

He carried no oar on his shoulder as he passed and spoke
no word to the shadow I was and I saw
what I thought was the face
of a ghost in his.

It was no face but a man's and that good enough to hold
the worms of starlight as he sailed home
on sodden sneakers that squished.

I followed and saw how he imagined nothing in the world
save the crabs he caught and now
carried where he lived
in that rolled and rotting paper bag
I would find abandoned everywhere in my life.

He thought: crabs again. And late, too.
I thought: what good is the imagination if it lies?

In memory now I cut through that same silky grass of summer,
wake-parted, feeling again the nightcrawlers
hidden like pieces of light underfoot.
I am dreaming the local
genius of my place.

Tycho Brahe, Newton, Poe—what were they to him?
He stepped under the stars with all that he knew
in his face and in the bottomless bag.

Through his yellow home-window I watched the tired heave of him,
that sea-wrinkled face dark as an apple,
as he dragged up to the table.
Here he had crawled and now

the old woman appeared and she put the crab
red as blood to steam in his moon-white platter.

I saw her kiss lightly the salted shell of neck,
her hand rubbing his head like a child's.

I, who could have been their son, hero of their dreams, stood
in the worm-riddled dark I invented.
I watched him speak the grace.
I saw how she sank there
beside him, luminous
while he ate.

IV. A Dream of Poe
Speaking in New York

Worked over here, I was badly screwed.
2 a.m., I leave the bar and walk as a man
hating his passion. She comes, bemused,
inescapable, dark, within:

working off the smell of them, that's the problem.
First steps light, but soon queasy,
street glistening like phlegm,
then rain plummeting.
                    Almost, it washes you
clean, so sudden and total is it.
In an X-rated theater I take refuge,
observing enormous tits.

Odd, I think of Helen, my dove.
She was all skittery as the street
and nearly as flat. But love
is for flesh, and flesh reeks.

              The light here is blue
and fizzles up that history, her drift
like blood's bubble, that *j'accuse*
in which sodden, beshit

in Baltimore, I lay shivering and stunned.
I try to forget the years, her, her pleas,
her sentimental hand, tongue
nothing now, nor knees

              lately loved and true,
for all it matters, that rivet
raw below, blistering, the brute
bed-dent after. Of children bereft,

I had none except her, my bride, who is gone.
She was brave, and I have been weak.
Is the world only scum?
Somewhere she sleeps.
                    I walk late. I watch lewd
movies. I am the dark one's instrument.
They speak to me of what I might do
to affront the black moment.

And rain falls as if to swallow everyone.
There is no innocence. Eternity
is New York, alone,
burning and ashamed. I dream

            no more than I always knew.
The ballad of flesh is never different.
And Death is no great virtue,
it is merely perfect.

For flesh offers only obligations and perfumes,
but Death is our vocabulary.
It is all I can speak to you.
Love is poisoned honey.

            I thought to find a way through
song to a far world painless and secret,
with pure women as static as truth.
Instead I am condemned to visit

each pit and sinkhole and sty and mausoleum
where love is. I do it eternally.
I reek of its smell, am almost human,
exiled to lust perpetually.

V. The End of Everything

How it glints out where least expected, the pink
spread of dawn light
in clots of ice

where the milk-horse of the past habitually broke through
the night's crust.

          I have got up with the air in my throat

blooming, shouldering up its white stalk.
My love, indolently lying
behind me in that fragrant bed,

remarks on "the shining body of the world."

And there, greasy, over the windowsill,
the mushrooming first light
(at first red as bougainvillaea)

          silently crawls along the naked

street where the horse once stood huffing,
nearly invisible, its spine
shattering the starlight,

a jeweler's blade
cracking loose a final fire.

There it is, running double-rutted, a pulse
intermittent, ectoplasmic.

          Now on elbows, keeping my nightmarish face

outside the room where she stirs to silk,

I speak of the great pink-orange orchid
of the future,
serenely, soundlessly sucking the breath to its singular bloom.

VI. Steamer to Baltimore

Tonight, watching the stars at the bow,
my head draped over with giddy blood,
body and boat drifting that other sky,
I think of you suspended in the Chesapeake
channel where wind frets and the seahawk
blinks over cordgrass.
                    You believed
in the black eyes of love that wait
beyond the deep rotting of the sea. I
have ridden out in this ancestral scow
to dream with you. Look at me
staring off over the tide's dark
as we pass through each humping swell.
This is the ghost's road to Baltimore.
The engines churn, the raked hull broods.

Men With/Without Women

Long after the first explosions of fear,
after the risen nodules, the swelling
under those uplifted arms that
in memory and distance now are
rubied as city stoplights, I see
her red hair hanging. It is morning
there where her voice sang like fire
in the wood-dark of the long hall.
I ran, breaking a string of Christmas
cards, to hear that pain that was not
pain yet, but would be after the fear
calling from the room where she stands.

This is the fatherless house that is nowhere.
Through the burst, violent sunlight
glare-filling that place once more
I enter her song and squint, and she,
like a ballerina, is scalding the air
I can scarcely breathe. In her mirror
she twirls into herself as in prayer.
The purple skirt halts above her ankles
white and tiny on the hardwood, not
white as her breasts with their red
stars. And now the boy I am blinks
at his mother nakedly crying, but cannot

speak, cannot help, all words gone dead
as iris bulbs under the winter ice.
The room flames. He watches light gather
itself around the world's astonishing
body, each muscle invariably coiled
on its dark seed, but to him only
shy, gorgeous as unutterable days
that would dream him into the dizzied
blood-rush of love. He tries not to see
how the world is turning, its arc
like the old mare trying to buck him.
He is only a boy, and knee-weak.

43

She knows he is not yet twelve, but man
enough to know what is happening,
to stand in front of raging glass
and hear her voice, oddly deep
in her throat, try to fling off
the fear, saying *See! See!* Her arms
lift all to him, riding high over
her bright red hair. What is it
he should see, blinded by the world?
They stand there like stumps, brushfire
crackling, turning all slowly black.
I knew their names. They were happy.

He would remember her tall window, dusk
come, and the hawk sailing, a cut
against the far sun-flame. And she,
without dressing and in her tears,
had sweetly gathered him in to sing
for the first star. Always its clear
scathing ice brought back her song,
even after the day fire surged
and his mare burned into cinders
that now, over the world's corpse,
swirl down in the winter's first snow.
I went, as boys do, to hide in the rocks

what that man in me already knew, the smoke
still rising from each scut, and ran
far off, or think that I did, though
all seems at this distance no more
than that sun-glare in her room.
Where did I go on that cold walk
of no return, under knots of stars
blooming endlessly in the high dark?
Of course I returned, the doctor's
shrill whistling called. He told me
I must break bread for her. In pieces
it lay uneaten, a skiff on her plate.

All night, now, in the city snow comes, and red
beacons of ploughs come, the memory
that cuts at the heart like hawks
seen far away and whirling. They scrape
the white from the long black land.
And maybe look up and see a boy standing
to see what stars say as their steel
blades break through to grind and ache.
Maybe they hear the *What?* she doesn't answer.
Or is this only the mind's ugly *Why?*
trying not to remember a brightness there,
and stars, later, shocking, promised?

45

A Day with No Clouds

There was a moment when someone, a gnat droning
into the pink of his eye, blinked.

The world loomed up then out of the grass.
Unfettered sun arced from window to window,
glissades of light took each green stem.

Out of hulls the insects had left,
crisp and sleek as a pine's needle,
the dreams of everything sang back to him.

In wooden buckets the well's black water
blistered the old lips. The air shone.

This was the moment of the man
who heard the night crack above a woman's breast.
He remembered the glacial fury of lightning,
how he had blinked like an owl when the world shook.

He turned his head slowly now, shielding his eyes
that morning. He heard the snail's packing,
a flurry of wings, the snap of far grass.

And then there was no wind. It was heart-still.
In what budless flower, in what crevice
was that other life?

He blinked. What was before flew from his eye.

His town's walls trembled its wash of light still.
It fell on him like loveless memory.

He tried to walk but the air banged in his chest.
His lips kept trying to make a name.
They wrinkled and spit dust.

There was a moment. There had been a moment.
Her hand came cool and rain-skittery on his face.
Before the sun sizzled. Before memory.

Under Dogwood, Under Pine, Under Spruce

That house crow-black in moonlight, the larder
of owls, the hawk's line shack, the blurred faces
staring from stones of the cracked foundation,
are these the miracles sworn to by wind
that rakes the night's cheek, the roof's lip?
Why does the lizard, eye-round and livid,
hang on each underedge, as if remembering?
And the tin cans toppled in crusts of snow
at dogwood, what lives have entered there?
The green body of the pine shakes and flares
its great shawl behind this abandoning,
as if ecstasy or a child had burst through.

Just down the hill a tongue of bronze water
lolls in a deep ditch, clotting the limbs
stitched together by a lost storm. Who
made this life? Who, watching the ribboned
dusk begin to shred on a window's wreckage,
sank teeth into a red lip and longed to hear
what would always hurt, that far stutter
of hope? Is she named by the iron thing flung,
leaving its red stain at the skirt of spruce
that always gave its lank shade to rain-barrel?
What questions, answers are held in the nave
of light you could wake to here when trees
begin to sway and ache? What words came
falling to freeze these walls and send a vine
folding into itself, and whose the endless
dream we step into, always, just off our path?

for Terry Hummer

Oak Leaves: Three Dreams

UTAH PROSPECTIVE

Dusk, and the raw wound almost invisible now,
for snow swirls and leans in ticking wind.
The obligations of grace have bled
from floral ribbons tattered, iced, like hair.

In the great gaunt oak by the chuchyard,
his dwelling place, the snow owl blinks
steadily as a man checking his watch.
Death's dreamer, his tongue is meaty, red, and wet.

THE SINNER

Spring has come and I think of you,
the hand writes. But why should this hand
tremble as it moves across the vacant page?
It cannot speak of any touch at night.
It rasps and stutters like a wind.
Yet this hand has cupped cold water
from a lost well and held it to lips
that let water fall and darken clay.
It held that face once and drew back
a cloth of leaves where a livid eye
blazed at the sun, then pitilessly sank
into memory. Habitual, it tries to return
to that well, as lovers did, before silence
came, and conspiring snow. That water
they dropped in the dark world was ice
by morning, a cold glintless skin
on the contracted earth. In it, a red
leaf with an eye waited to thaw.
Like a hand it seemed to tremble.
Like a hand unable to be given or withdrawn.

49

OAK LEAF, A MIDNIGHT DREAM

It rained, long strings that nippled the ground
by her tall gray house, and I lay in a flood.
Then the hard creak of a rocker came
and the voice that is no voice

in this life came. I had not wanted to find that
rocker hunched against the wall, the sky
rolling over the loud oak, but went
to stand beside it. Red leaves showered

beyond the window, like a blood-rush in high wind,
like a stranger come, in desperation, long
after the hour the house would be shut.
I went and stood but was not

the boy called from a dark window, nor the lover
I had been once, leg-cracked under the oak.
This time I had not fallen, in silence,
like the down-droop of a clock's hand.

I was only the slow seep and trickle of a presence
as untranslatable as the shaken gestures
of an oak leaf whose veins would be,
at first light, lucid

and clear as her skin under silk and lace. The oak
rose in my dream, stripped, familial, hurt,
and the chair in no wind I could feel
went on rocking and rocking.

Probably in some vestigial ditch of the night,
flesh fevered, her crying finished,
she waits. Or has just gone
to buy the ticket to Tulsa,
by Greyhound and local carrier,
and does not think of the man who,
once, I was, the lean boy that fled
unscratched by the great stars
that scarcely notice us.
Probably she wept at seeing
the pure bright pearl of semen that dried
to a crust on the last stocking she owned.

How should a good girl go home, even where no home
is, legs naked, and wind ever cold?
Or maybe the enormous moon
howls through a window where
one yellow jonquil flakes
in her eyes and falls like a leaf
gold down the black well's throat,
that sudden and bottomless place.
It is her memory. The rain rings
but cannot wash away what happened
where a bucket hung and hands, the first,
went spidery under skirts lifted from her legs.

It might even be that she remembers nothing at all.
If the world forgets all we have done.
There is that chance. Her face boils
around the storm-staggered radio
where she lives. Maybe all she wants
is our manic country's heart
to forgive itself. This song
goes on trying to explain nakedness,
its lips drumming on the velvet
of her belly. It comes from Tulsa.

Her clothes, with her name sewn inside,
wait in supermarket bags, as she files herself.

All of her stories are true, and nobody's business.
She makes them up so she will know
she is real. But how can you tell
in the wind and the rain, alone?
The notes try to clatter through
and its seems she does not dream
but is dreamed by the jonquil.
Still as a lover's face it looks,
and she feels the root-knot
long to burst from its brown cage.
It will die, watered to death.
Why has she tried to keep it in the world?

Why has she, in this moment, had to rise up and go
to the window with its rivulets of faith?
Doll-placid, hair lank with rain,
she dressed herself at the sink.
The dress is silver lamé, like stars,
and will shimmer on the dirt road.
Now, with the last radio's
crackle, the room turns farmhouse
where naked feet sleepily shuffle.
At stair's landing, in a ticking pool,
she straps on her patent slippers
and begins to walk, head buried in the news.

Walks as if in dew and only to the deep well.
Dogwood made her skin pink and sweet.
She knows her name. Who else knows?
Maybe he is there, or will be soon,
who once sang her the sun and called
her Baby. Her hands fell down.
She couldn't know how furious love

might be in a person, how it
nailed on your lips those names
that weren't anyone's. She'd use them,
use whatever she had until it flaked dead,
and all softened again and time came to go home.

for Richard Schramm

They came down to the small pier, submerged, where our rowboat
dangled on a tether of rope and gathered water once.
Moonlight raised some of the boards. Their feet,
as they walked out, glistened and seemed to dance.

We could not hear their love step on the light surface
but saw them lean and sway and glint, night-swallows
we said, though we knew their names, the blessed
look of lovers walked beyond sun's blistering glow.

Then they were gone, and the planks drifted somewhere.
Why do we lean after them when they are not real,
when we are certain the heart can bear no more
reality, or even the ocean's blue everpresent squeal?

The random pulse and impulse of the sea comes soft
but has been hard and houses here have been broken.
We throw more wood on the fire and watch a draft
from far out swirl smoke in as if some word, spoken,

comes back across the dark slick to answer itself.
Light ripples just beyond the surf, where the pier ends,
and may be only their tossed beer can that drifts.
Why do we love this wreckage with no intent?

We think we hear him remark to her, enigmatically, on
action, reaction, the predictable odds of survival
love has against this world. Then they are gone,
the conversation is ours, the yearning to be, to feel

the rhythm that grinds the flesh of the shore is ours.
At first we fill the quiet room with speculation,
screeching like gulls, eyes yellow with fire.
We invent what is, was, will be, their destination,

a room under a white shawl of pine, sand and a long kiss.
The night grows baffling and the moon lies breast-white
as a footpath of joy in the sea. It invites us
to forget the fire that flakes and stutters in dry-

rotted wood we picked from the tide piece by piece.
We saw them, the shadows of a man and a woman,
but who were they? We mean, who are we?
Exhausting the possibilities we drive ourselves on

until the darkness in the east begins its looming gray.
Now there is only shoreline, tide going, black
stumps of pier rising in collapse, two gulls splayed
rigidly above the lipped, red horizon of the Atlantic.

We remember the lost rowboat, the first days in this house,
but were they real, the lovers? What evidence?
We breathe the cold where we live, the fire out,
our voices low, cracked, barely whispering of love rent.

Was first that you had a flat tire, so stopped
on the street known so well that it never
had to have a name. Still,
it looked like nowhere you were, ever,
when someone whose face
caught in the light an odd instant
honking, calling you *Fool!*
It seemed to say, but did not,

I can't live without you.

Squatting in the traffic and heat, the haze
of July like a raw memory
timed for distant explosions,
you sagged out of breath, steamed,
and felt, now, wildly open.
To think of old tracers, the maze
of ribboned, silent phosphorous
from guns that set the Pacific ablaze—

the sea had not felt violent at all
under your feet, under shuddering tons
of U.S. Navy steel, but gentle,
though treachery could stun
anytime, anywhere. It rose in
that cruddy hubcap, and appalled,
where eyes were the same full
blue from the other life, a total

shock like negatives found, undeveloped:
hers, yours. That was the second thing,
buried until now, the hubcap
banging on the curb, its ring
only a small concussion
but enough to wake you up,
then the truck's backfire, a black
terror unsuspected, but kept.

And that third wound, the gouge, red,
small blood on your knuckle
that you sucked at so tears
wouldn't come and that buckle
in your knees wouldn't happen
(though it did, oh God, it did)
as cars flowed back and forth until
you beat on the goddamned steel and cried

I can't live without you.

IGNORANCE

Darkness, except for the yellow night-light in the hall
and, in bed, blink of the eyes like a hammer.
And out there the murderous morning's truck
screeches someone to work, and the world is back.
The eyes flare open. She is, perhaps, something better,
sweating it out now, cough gone, though color appalls.

That is the season I think of, wherever it happened, place
immaterial and time of no consequence, my heart zooming
in fatigue and fear. That sickness ended, ends each
time it comes, but I keep the memory and reach
through it to what is worse, that first morning
we walked from a house locked in ice, that precise face

we left inside, and the feverish instructions it bequeathed.
What were they? Innocuous words about good, loving other
than self, grandmotherly nostrums. We saw how late
blue spilled, how dawnlight would go gray and flat,
and spears of the indifferent ice were going to shatter,
but we remarked, numbly, on the weather, choking grief

with efficient calculations. Pragmatists, the future
said bury and be done. Perhaps that is why
a small stunned body leads me to that time
I stood in the yard and did not debate your scheme
of assets and obligations. Dew crunched underfoot and I
paced there a long time, then someone called, dark in the door.

MOCKINGBIRD

In the mulberry tree behind the interlacing pines
the mockingbird shrieks against silence.

Frost muffles whitely the least of breath
as I watch the dark door, but I hear
the crackle of that birdcall. I know it
is the sound I make trying to recreate
the moment before silence shatters.
I want the world's possible gray light.
It is my own voice, I think, darkly preening.
And the door has not opened. I must be silent
to hear that thrown other voice from the darkness.

COMPUTER ANALYST,
AMERICAN REALISM

So the baby came because, well you know,
the answer to that, the tape's antecedent,
like a high pressure combining with a low.
The result is SNAFU, is a storm, a rent

in the banked way of life you engendered.
Isn't that how you put it one night?
What was the weather? Was it entered?
Probably not. Only getting up, the light

sickened in your face, then the heart-knot.
They said it was no one's fault, of course.
Even she said that. It was just what you got,
the program, and it could have been worse.

So you buried baby and life was the same
as always. You went to numbers and came back.
Trees were trees, sometimes it rained.
It was hard to tell dreams from facts

and after a while you no longer tried.
Whoever you were, the world forgot.
No one you knew grew happy, no one died,
or imagined they'd been lucky, or not.

An easy autumn day, the chill deceit skeletal
that will in the hard dark rake our bones.
For what have we heaved to raise the window?
We remember again the clank of lead inside
casements swollen tighter than memory's boil.
Was it only air we wanted, to cool love's bite?
Whose touch was the last? Then an instant light
leaped in our narrow space, we fell far back
to the adolescent gnawing, to a dreamed world
no words could cajole to a bidable shape.
Pure and perfect we lay in our rented sheets
and were what the dream had said, each to each.
Far below cars crawled like maggots, lightning
blundered over the water's distance like lies
we had not yet told but would, in whispers, tell.
We lay on the bed in that room of deep stains,
soon to sleep, wake, love, descend into the weeks
whose end, gathering, we'd lick like first rain
in our faces on each corner. And memory waited
hunched in the subway, in a face almost right
but not, withered and beaten in its shy glance.
So much the flesh will not see. In a cat-dark
hovel we shivered and yawned in indolent delight,
you quoting Lowell's *Dolphin* on lovers' ends,
"saying too little, then too much." Before dinner,
without words, ruthless, we did it again, acute
as a glassmaster's knife in a shop. Then dressed,
went down, fumbling the words that mattered, back
to Lowell, before parting, who was off with tears
gilding the world of rooms, of people like us.
I kept hearing the cabbie far off say *Where now?*

Something Is Missing

I do not have to because the world is full
of exotic and dangerous bridges but I
dream

  two little boards rickety as a tightrope

over a lagoon, and out there at the end
a real rope hanging in the glassy surface.
It is like love's one thread.
Probably there is a story

a hard-working man could tell you here, a weather
to make your eyes burn, the tart smell
of fruit, and this information

might rekindle some appetite you had.
If it appears you have been here, try to remember
you are in a dream and in dreams

something is always missing,

something which you are in position to supply.
That is the story I will not tell.

I want to warn you those planks are full of rot
and, while the water rises, to make you
understand there is no time
to hurry in dreams.

You
must take hold
sooner or later. The rope
hangs perfect as a postcard from another country.

Sax Man

Everything had sweat on it, a glistening like spittle,
the kind of slide dreams make, but a real world
where I went, quiet as a bat, only to sing
inside myself, to pass time, to be no more
than a slight thing in the night's wind.

But not wind and I, under the constant chaos of that dark,
hung on the ledge of my love like a dragonfly.
Have hung that way with my dark, shattered eye

full of the horrible hours scaling inside like a baby's
first trip up and down the notes of his knowing.
It chiseled and kicked inside, the image
of her absence, and still I stood
on the flat slick of that time and blew in my hands
when it was not cold, and wanted to dart anywhere

but saw the first gusting firelick. Saw what was not there
and had no name for it but love, and for that leaped
and made in the dark what I wanted to be real, made
the burning that lay in the place of sight

on the lake's face. Did this with mouth dry as a callous
to draw out the song from the wimpling house
of my flesh, saw how it ran screaming

in a nakedness fuming which no one could touch but at pain.
Touched that, became a man whistling for menus,
stepped into the line of blind foreheads
where now I lie, note after note,
in the ditches of skin, building back what was
beautiful and malign as the slant of her whispering.

Homecoming Parade, That Music

What accounts for a man's delight is not only whisky poured
and the astonishing love in the bared heart
of the ex-cheerleader howling us home.

I have lain down among men and women again, happy, and wish
I may never rise up and not hear down the hall
love's wretching with surprised tears.
I have tumbled through a lovely town
shouting my blind fight song
from the bed of a truck
whose driver, a kind man,
said, slyly, do dance with my wife.

This morning I woke up dreaming that waltz into the dark
of quick and desperate breasts I can't even name.
And there, when I climbed from a guest's sofa,
the daughter of hosts, in transparent lace,
leaned at the household's huffing dryer.

Her red hair, angelic, scalds me
like the shower I could never control.

She, too, will learn how we grow small in foreign waters
and come home to badly sing our shattered songs.
How many times have we touched ourselves for her,
who is only what we dream
when delight and pain are one?

Toweling quickly, and alone, in suburban basements
we can hear the canned air-horns hooting
toward the crowded stadium.
They say: YOUR ATTENTION, PLEASE!

A farm wagon turned Roman chariot rolls
past, the girl you loved bouncing on your lap.
Your fake toga rises even now.

63

Through mist, her smile is like the sun stared at.

Amazed at what we are, I walk through sycamores
snowed by revelers with plenty of toilet paper, some pink.
I move like a farmboy, hungover, and pass
the majorette in sequins, her lank
looming mother.

Homecoming makes us all think of thighs soon to lift
in the forgotten gray of our towns,
that amazement of breath
everywhere held inside
about to burst with the promised joy.

The mother and you and I are saying wait, wait
but the horns hoot, but she says
Oh God, oh God it is
finally happening.

Before the long sleeping show windows, I come back
to stand among halters, napkins, and the memory
of one body whose hair twirled
for me by the quick river.
I'm shaved and reeking,
the car radio blasts
to the leveled soybean field, and
here she comes like the fine whip of a car antenna—

oh, risen!

I should be hundreds of home-miles away, climbing
on unstable kitchen chairs,
trying to screw
the fresh lightbulb in,
my shirt left with my son's glove
where he waits tossing the ball in the air.

I should turn my collar back down and remember the pain
the coach showed us that dark day
the projector broke, sores
like the first films
of the A-bomb in civics.

But I am licked by delight at the soft back of my knees,
and here she comes, stepping to that horn
tuned perfectly right, herself
leaping electrically,
with baton, and how can I help
running among the others
to seek out some new, wonderful angle?

I think of home, change jingling, and think I do not want
to come wordless and waiting in
the Purina Feedstore lot
but the road leads nowhere else,
and last night there was a face
in a night-blackened truck.
We called it love and it answered,
it drove us where we wanted to go.

Dressed only in a white sheet, disguised as our oldest dream,
whoever she may have been wanted a last dance
and I rose when she crooked a naked finger,
her whisper what no good man can resist,

Come here, now, and listen to the music.

---

for William Mills

65

October, that glittering rakehell month,
snorts in the bushes where the widow is
busy with weeds. They still defeat her.
With them she has trafficked for years,
but what if she, puttering, with rake,
with shears, should suddenly discover
her fingers have gone numb? On bent knees,
her face lifted so the black streaks
of earth seem time's batterings, she
may yet remember the high shrill stars
at the edge of summer and sing, for
behind them a darkness not earth parts
gently again and again. And if, then,
her brow in light sweat breaks to wear
the mask that runs to mud along bone,
let us lean close and watch and hear her
stab as deep as ever through the hours.
She was beautiful once and may be again.
In October the leaves are lipped in ice
but heat, like hope, lingers in flowers,
under nails, in the cleaving song she sings.

Elk Ghosts: A Birth Memory

Tirelessly the stream licks the world until
from snow they do not come, but are
hoof-deep and standing, silhouettes
stark on the stones under stars.

Gathered, they seek a way to reenter
paths graven on the bone-walls.
Their white breath is alive. It is
possible to walk into and out

of monstrous, gentle eyes, knowing no link
exists except your face anchored
in the herd's dream. They are beyond
stillness and memory, their

revelation the lapping fire-fleck of water
and the starbright lintel of stones.
They come here to wait for change,
to be dreamed among pine and spruce.

There is no hawk who could hook them
out of the blue they breathe
effortlessly. Each moon-swollen
needle leads them more into vision.

Time conspires with you at night's window
and cannot help but hope for this
birth of joy. No longer do they
wait, no more nuzzle the future.

They glide through desire on earth.
Their thin song has entered each reed,
it has risen in your sleep and wails
forth these white shadows

you have summoned. They become electric
in your blood. One after another
they bear the stars, walking on water,
beasts with backs of pure light.

There is no world they cannot carry.
They are love's magi. Hooves flare
with a way through the darkness.
Composed, they suffer your coming.

Juniper, Wyoming

The wind in silver snowswirls grazes
each withering thigh of pine, riffling
through small rocks, pockets of eyes,
through the few cones openly lying.
It eddies and polishes what has fallen
from the mountain's huge gray. Far off
the slowly shaking amber light holds
hawks, and the pool of the plains
shudders like an iced lake stepped on
the first time. It tightens its bite
along the Juniper's long down-lacing root.
Each morning a woman rubs her face
against the sound of what has been lost,
though all remains in the wind that goes
indifferently surging and scraping. Today
she saw the rabbit's throat, how white
under Juniper's shadow. When she slips
the robe off at night, her eyes lower,
knowing everything has waited for this,
feeling that tree tilt its naked brow
like a man watching for the no-light
when she will lie and say nothing
with hand on her mouth, rough as bark.

Up the hill the motorcycle climbs, its sound
near now, entering the dream,
and the girl's hair flares

because it is morning, because I have been sleeping
long enough to become one of the muscles
flexing beside the world's gristle.

I can feel the sheet luff on my thighs, the emptiness
cool and pleasant inside my body, and time
stops counting the spruce limbs.

I think this must be the silence that love always is,
except I can hear a dog barking, a big dog
far away, then his nails gouging dirt,

and I feel myself twist for the articulation to be free.
The little engine pumps hard, she hangs
on my shoulders, and we are not

going down in grinding of gravel, not this time, we are
filling silence with the two-stroke slide
of the morning and time rattles

like joy in the spruce, in the car-door slammed, the jay
spitting out the black, stale hours,
the sun flying over each bump

in the road, touching the essence of each thing until
the world ticks with unbearable delight,
slows, turns, and comes hard again.

This morning you came home with three.
Each is tagged, two maples, red bracelets,
the third in ragged yellow, a mulberry.
Now they are as tall as we project

our children, ten years grown, still thin
stalks of mottled bone, blandly naked.
Each wears a thatched top, leaves skimmed
by a little wind, hardly enough to rake

if it were raking season, and it isn't.
At the kitchen window, pausing over pots,
you wave me to dreamed arrangements.
I lift the tubs and waddle over the lot,

guessing what kind of shade we'll make.
Sometimes you speak, your lips moving
without words, lovely and pale, or shake
your head at the sun. It is then I think

what it might be, this home, cool, mapled,
but without you. Except you'd be here,
no matter how tall they grew, how dappled
by feverish light, how blitzed by winter.

At last you hold your hands up: it's done.
When I come in to look, they're triangular.
"Now dig," you say, "careful to root each one
with space to grow." Then, back to supper.

Tunneling like a mole, I stop and watch you
in the shell of the house, contentedly cooking.
These trees will stand long at your window,
and larks, as if I put them there, sing

71

back this moment and moments yet undreamed.
Rooting deep, I am buried in our future,
in flags of maple and fruit of mulberry,
that gently to my hands you delivered.

Wedding Song

Camden, North Carolina, is not picturesque
though it is the place we remember
where many men and women have gone
in good luck and bad to repair
aching hearts: for five bucks
no one asks your age or looks for the curve

swelling under the skirt of the cheerleader.
Our justice of the peace pumped gas
and spoke the words through gums
long toothless and tobacco black.
A tourist honked for help.

He gave each of us a sample box of Cheer.
Y'all come on back anytime!

The first time down Route 17, by George Washington's
ditch, he of the chopped cherries,
we turned back in the Dismal Swamp.
Who could make up a truer thing than that?

You weren't fooling. Neither was I.
Believe this now: neither was I.
The second time we made it.
But without some jokes
who could bear
love's roaring?

A wheezing clerk above an X-rated movie house
slowly printed our names.
He chewed an onion's golden rings.
He said, *Are you now or have you ever been crazy?*

Weren't we? Isn't love something that breaks,
drooling and dangling inside
like a hot-water hose
that leaves you helpless and godforsaken?

73

Y'all come on back anytime.
Fifty bucks and two economy boxes of Cheer—
how far could we get on that?

I was certain you'd end up croaking home
to mother after those early months.
Our first house had more holes
than we could cover, mice,
snakes, spiders, our dinner guests.

It was there you woke in the screams of a mare
who dropped half of her foal, dragging
half around our rented house
until with a tractor and chain
our landlord delivered us.

The chain still dangles in your dream,
and his *Y'all come back anytime.*

Sometimes when I think we have learned
to live in the world, the faces
of children lining our walls,
the darkness waiting ahead
like a swamp that's no joke,

I turn and find you coiled in a corner of light.
I think of the five green dollars unfurled
for that clerk of fat gold and fools,
the blue acrid soap
that scoured us cherry red,
and the screams of the years.

Are we now or were we ever crazy?
Sign here, the man said, and we did,

the voices of men and women,
for pleasure,
riding up through
that black ancient floor.

I hear them still.

---

for Dee

Sometime We Will Ride into Saint Louis

NIGHT OF THE CHICKENS,
NORTH OF JOPLIN

Whiskey would not do to unremember all the nights
where, with her, you lay down quiet,
thinking the sun beautiful
in its last hovering, in sycamores,
but a man can't lie or keep as he wants
far out of the world's push. North, then,

and East, the hard cold of Kansas or Arkansas against
windows open because it always gets too hot,
your hand like a child's out there
flapping in the surge, thinking
probably it was like this for your father
prone under the B&O boxcars—except
his fingers had clamped on the rods,
the fear in his mouth set so he
couldn't lose the Irish
even when pried out and beaten.

Once, passing a small cloud in the dimming horizon,
you think of your mother bedding down
and can't recall her name,
or even the name of the girl left,
and though it ought to be easy
to shake off the memory of old love,
that cloud brings back its absence
and the hot light.
                    Night comes,
your car glides like the moon's river,
then the curve, the skid, for God's sake,
chickens that seem to want to die, and do,
in timeless explosions, absurdly breaking

both headlights.
                    Now there is only feeling

79

the road, no more blundering
through hummocks of darkness, now
the blind crawl from houselight
to houselight, sometimes speeding
to trail a car that passes, the hope
you might steal his taillight and limp in.

It doesn't work. He looks back in fear.
This late no one can help and the world
lies as lonely as an empty bed
on Christmas Eve, except

the kid in the loud Ford will still blindside you,
almost, and the girl wrapped around him
laugh as they ghost into the night.
Stung, fatherless this trip,

heaving toward home but with no country yours
or even more than a black space,
there is nowhere to go, only
the going, engine steady

and absurd as the chickens dead in Missouri.
In everything there is this
necessary foolishness of love,
his letter said, and the funerals
of fathers.
To get through, drive hard,

sing a chorus for each roadhouse, each sleepy ghost.
Sing for a girl's thigh in moonlight,
for the dark you roar down in.
Sing for the dawn that crusts
ice-bright on your windshield,
the gold glow she lies in without you.

Leave the windows open to cry out.
Turn on the radio, check the time.
Imagine how he flew inches
above the razoring gravel,
her name in his head like a country.
In this country everyone is strange.

---

for Michael Heffernon

SOMETIMES I THINK I WILL RIDE INTO SAINT LOUIS

It is like that some nights, the fine weave
of everything unraveled at last.
The eyes, like blisters, run
red, white and raw under the moon
that picks out an oak's naked limb
to wave over the highway
like a thick, low snake
saying PAY ATTENTION.

The deja vu comes then, driving again.
The moon's long glare washes you
back to a field in mist coiling
white as your bride's slip.
What happened there?
Memory abandons you, but
not desire, and at
seventy you touch her face.

Would whiskey help the unremembering?
You went to him once, nothing you could do.
Still, you told them, a little
drink in a jelly glass,

an old man's heart
can stand that much, can't it?

Who were you to deny his love? So poured,
and have poured as you rolled
all day alongside the freights.

At the overlook, both of you drinking from a paper bag,
she said what the hell, why not
do what he would have done,
just go?
        So did,

exactly, and got married in some god-awful gloomy pit,
wound up reciting Yeats to the hare-lip
at the Ozark Amoco, before dawn,
which she, yawning, claimed was cruel,
and was, no matter it got you through
the water-pump's burst bowels,

no matter he said Crazy Jane to his relief man.

Flying through Missouri again, easterly light risen
like lead in your face,
the night tattering out everywhere
like a hopeless man in longjohns,
there they were, the shacks
men live in, one standing
who might scratch or fry bacon
but would not be your Irishman
bellowing love
like a pledge of allegiance.

Though a countryman, maybe, having come into Saint Louis
like a katydid clutching steel,
and the stars,

82

for sweet Mary's sake,
enough to break a poor man's heart.

A little drink before he dies, not so bad a thing,
you were thinking, when she
opened her eyes and it could not happen
again, what you had told her, but
she screamed too late to stop
the skid into the farmer's crate-filled truck.

Never mind how the world ends, it greets you
with what you can't predict.
Except you can.

Chicken feathers float in the mind like love's hair
stuck to the cold rails of freights,
they float in the brown whiskey
where stars, son, forever shine,
and sometimes you make it
and just have to sing.

Stay off the whiskey and try hard to love her
whom you love, for she is a man's
comfort, and all there is.

Dented and beaten and chicken-bruised, sometimes
you make it and hear her laugh,
Oh God tell me you love me.

And just as you do, the sun
explodes in the great arch
its round foolish blister of joy
as if this were all you had come for.

And it is.